KT-375-010

12/11 #1

Evo 10 Time 1.28.2
Best Lap Time 1.36.2

BUT RUBBISH!

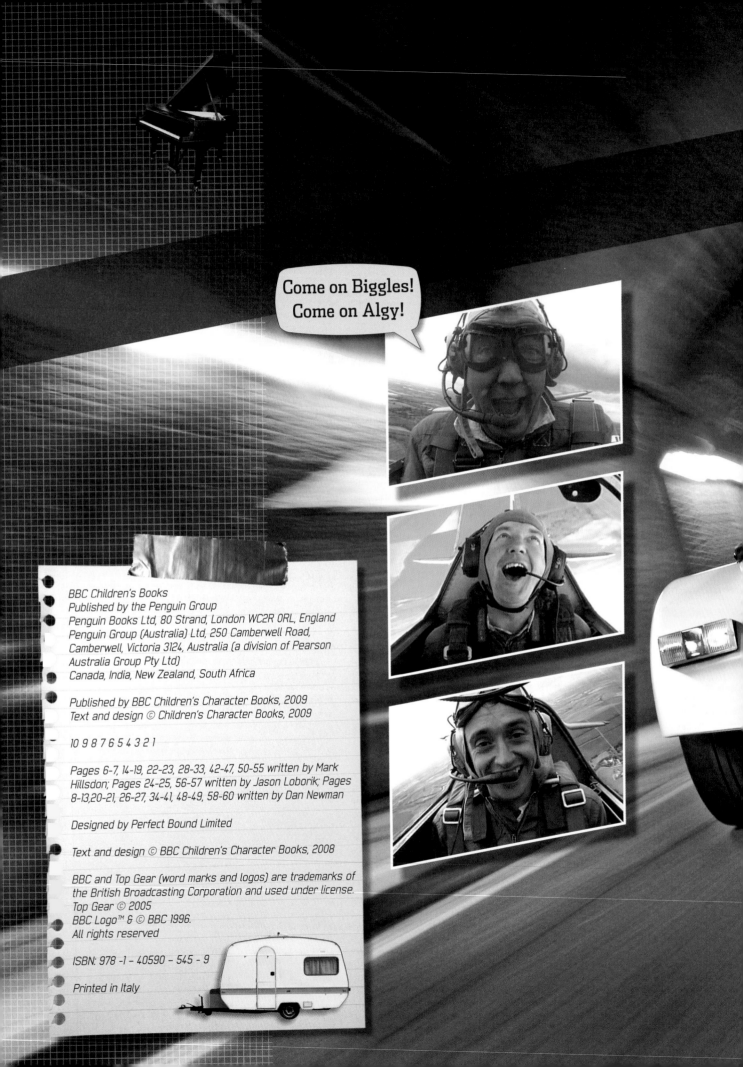

Come on Biggles!
Come on Algy!

BBC Children's Books
Published by the Penguin Group
Penguin Books Ltd, 80 Strand, London WC2R 0RL, England
Penguin Group (Australia) Ltd, 250 Camberwell Road,
Camberwell, Victoria 3124, Australia (a division of Pearson
Australia Group Pty Ltd)
Canada, India, New Zealand, South Africa

Published by BBC Children's Character Books, 2009
Text and design © Children's Character Books, 2009

10 9 8 7 6 5 4 3 2 1

Pages 6-7, 14-19, 22-23, 28-33, 42-47, 50-55 written by Mark
Hillsdon; Pages 24-25, 56-57 written by Jason Loborik; Pages
8-13, 20-21, 26-27, 34-41, 48-49, 58-60 written by Dan Newman

Designed by Perfect Bound Limited

Text and design © BBC Children's Character Books, 2008

ISBN: 978 -1 - 40590 - 545 - 9

Printed in Italy

CONTENTS

How many Stigs?

All the way through this annual there are pictures of the Stig. Your task, if you can be bothered, is to count them all. We've had a go, and our answer is on page 61. (Tip: that's NOT the back of his head above, driving the Caterham R500.)

Meet the Team

It's been a hectic couple of series for the Top Gear team, who've had to drag their weary bodies halfway round the world to bring you adventure and excitement from the likes of America, Japan and Vietnam.

As ever they've all experienced their own highs and lows, so before you wade into another action-packed annual, here's a quick refresher on what the lads got up to!

ARRGGHHHHH!

Jeremy Clarkson

Poor Jezza has been through the wars a bit, ricking his neck while testing the Nissan GTR, and suffering an unfortunate accident with a gear stick during the truck challenge. He even managed to lose his voice, which was pretty careless of him!

But he also got to grips with some great cars, from the menacing Mercedes Black to a Corvette ZR1 and the Lamborghini Gallardo. But he had most fun in a humble Ford Fiesta, which he thrashed round the inside of a shopping centre before helping the Royal Marines out with an amphibious beach assault!

The perfect gift: a first aid kit
Don't mention: the gear stick of a Renault Magnum

Richard Hammond

Cruising along the French Riviera in a Ferrari Daytona was a top highlight for the Hamster, as was testing the 'catastrophically ugly' Gumpert Apollo. He also managed to take the new Caterham for a spin and dramatically won a race in a Bowler Wildcat against his German counterpart.

Although he had less success behind the wheel of a truck, Richard did drive his VW BlueMotion to victory in the One Tank Challenge, and saw the future of motoring when he took Toyota's i-REAL car/chair for a drive.

The perfect gift: the keys to a Ferrari Daytona
Don't mention: Japanese food

Ye gods – this is something else!

Have a Scandinavian flick, Finnish person!

James May

James also took a bit of a battering in the last two series and ended up with a bruised bum after crashing through the waves in his powerboat. He was also ruthlessly rammed off the road by Jeremy in his Morris Marina.

But there were happier times for Captain Slow in America, where he fell in love with his Cadillac, and also in Finland where he learnt the Scandinavian Flick from motorsport god, Mika Hakkinen. And he even managed to win the Truck Challenge – although the competition wasn't too fierce!

The perfect gift: a Finnish phrase book
Don't mention: the Tokyo train system

The Stig

Another dramatic year for the Stig, in which we learnt that he may well have invented the month of November, has a full size tattoo of his face, on his face, and can't wear socks. It was also rumoured that he sleeps inside out.

On the test track he was at his breath-taking best, setting a new record time of 1 minute 17.1 in the Gumpert Apollo, while he also enjoyed himself at Blackpool Pleasure Beach. He was, apparently a bit embarrassed though when we got to meet his cousin Rig Stig, during the Truck Challenge!

The perfect gift: a season ticket to Blackpool Pleasure Beach
Don't mention: being caught on camera underneath a yellow umbrella. It did nothing for his street cred!

AMERICAN MUSCLE

★★★★★★★

Is there any point to big, fat, crude, cheap American muscle cars? Jeremy, James and Richard flew to California to have a serious and STRICTLY factual look at three new beasts.

★ The cars

In San Francisco (14th biggest city in America – **FACT**) they picked up their cars. Jeremy got a Corvette ZR1, James had a Cadillac CTS-V and Richard got... nothing. Chrysler wouldn't lend him a Dodge Challenger because they thought he would be horrid about it. In order to stay strictly factual, he went out and bought one – with his own money!

They drove over the Golden Gate Bridge (opened in 1927 – **FACT**) and along some freeway (American for motorway – **FACT**). James quickly decided he didn't like the Caddy – he felt it was too powerful for what is meant to be a relaxed, stylish sedan.

★ Corvette ZR1
Engine: 6.2 litre supercharged V8
Power: 640bhp
0-60mph: 3secs
Max. speed: 205mph
Cost: $100,000 – a lot for a Corvette

★ Dodge Challenger
Engine: 6.1 litre V8
Power: 425bhp
0-60mph: 5.1 secs
Max. speed: over 170mph
Cost: Richard paid $51,000, 10K more than normal

★ Cadillac CTS-V
Engine: 6.2 litre supercharged V8
Power: 556bhp
0-60mph: 3.9secs
Max. speed: 191mph. The fastest four-door saloon, apparently

They're like **killer whales.** They're ver **striking** to look at and **very fast.** But you wouldn't want t **own one.**

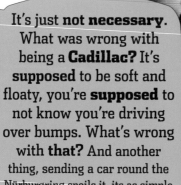

It's just **not necessary.** What was wrong with being a **Cadillac?** It's **supposed** to be soft and floaty, you're **supposed** to not know you're driving over bumps. What's wrong with **that?** And another thing, sending a car round the Nürburgring spoils it, its as simple as that. I can see exactly why the

★★★★★ ★★★★★

> I **love** muscle cars. They're about cowboy boots, denim jeans, dime stores... I **love** that. I'm feeling **cooler** already.

> It's not **supposed** to be a Rolls Royce. It's **simple**, it's **fast** – it's a **worker's car.**

> Are you 'born in the USA?'

> It's like a **bodybuilder** – hugely impressive, but when you take its **trunks** down...

Jeremy, of course, gets the muscle car thing: The noise it made pulling away almost made him non-factual. 'Hah-haah! That is intoxicating. Errr... I'm not being entertaining, I'm just saying, that is really incredible.' However, he felt it was too brash and ghastly for Britain.

Hammond was utterly overexcited about his Dodge because, deep down, he *is* American.

★ The looks

At Lake Tahoe (eighth deepest lake in the world – **FACT**) Jeremy and James teased Richard about his Dodge being all style and no substance, with pretend carbon fibre and ram airscoops that didn't do anything.

Mind you, Jeremy's car had its fair share of cheap bits; a pointless window in the bonnet, and a back end made of the same plastic Americans use to make newsreaders. But what could you expect from something made in Kentucky by two fat men called Bob?

That night they got to Reno, a smaller, tackier version of Las Vegas. James tried very hard to win a car on the fruit machines – ANY car – while Jeremy and Richard got dangerously close to being entertaining, by revving their immense engines to set off car alarms. The police soon set them back on the factual track.

> My **foot** slipped off the **clutch**.

> No sir, I don't buy that for a **second**.

★ The desert

The next day didn't find James in a better mood, as he was still stuck with the Cadillac. They took Highway 50, the loneliest road in America, which goes in a straight line through the desert. For hours. They got so bored, Jeremy started counting the stitches in the door.

After six years (**NOT** a fact) they stopped for breakfast. Jeremy played a non-factual prank on Richard by moving the Dodge, using its 'Keyless Go' feature.

This is the **best** American car I've **ever** driven!

My car was **there** and now its **there**! How the – that's **weird**.

When they finally got out of the desert, they took a twisty road through the mountains. And – miraculously – James finally started to like his car. In fact, he really, really loved it.

Jeremy was similarly enthusiastic. 'How can a car as docile as this one is, most of the time, be this exciting?

Well done, fat men from Kentucky! This is a masterpiece!' James even overtook Jeremy, as he was in the way.

They drove off through the spectacular hills, but sadly the filming had to stop as they were almost being entertaining.

He's **really** shifting now, is Captain Slow!

★ ★ ★ ★ ★ ★ ★ ★ ★ ★ ★ ★ ★ ★ ★ ★ ★

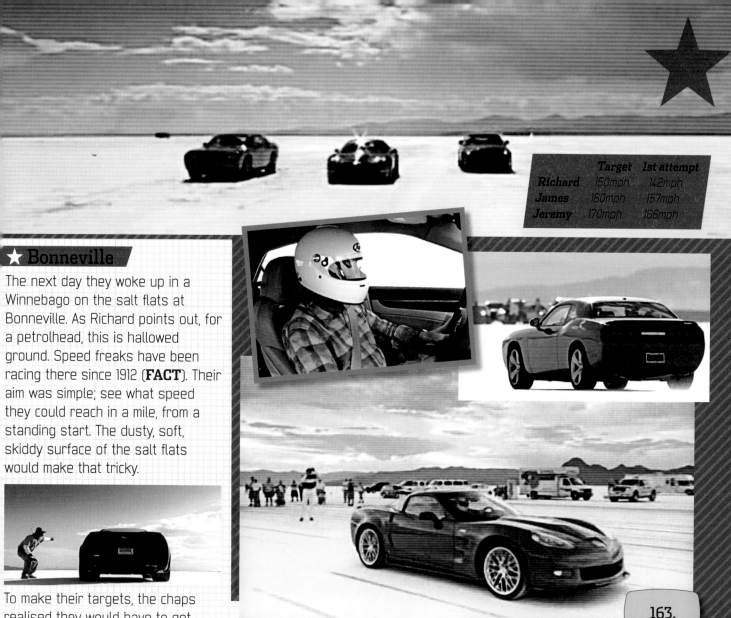

	Target	1st attempt
Richard	150mph	142mph
James	160mph	157mph
Jeremy	170mph	166mph

★ Bonneville

The next day they woke up in a Winnebago on the salt flats at Bonneville. As Richard points out, for a petrolhead, this is hallowed ground. Speed freaks have been racing there since 1912 (**FACT**). Their aim was simple; see what speed they could reach in a mile, from a standing start. The dusty, soft, skiddy surface of the salt flats would make that tricky.

To make their targets, the chaps realised they would have to get every single aspect of their driving exactly right. Which was going to be very hard. Jeremy managed the fastest time ever recorded at Bonneville for a production car, but he still wasn't happy. 'Damn, damn, damn, damn, damn!' James got remarkably competitive, pushing in front of Jeremy for another go. 'I like this game,' he said.

Jeremy and James tried pumping their tyres up, while Richard was advised to let some air out. He got the wrong advice. Jeremy and James got within 1mph of their target; Richard was back down at 139mph.

Next time he pumped them right up, taped up the radiator grille to improve the aerodynamics ... and made it! 150.02mph.

Pumping his tyres up to the point of bursting, Jeremy gave it everything and hit 176 mph. Would James make it three out of three? It looked good, it felt good and ... it was good.

Richard emerged from the Honey Bucket (portable toilet – **FACT**) to get the good news.

163.

Yess!

We've **all** hit our target!

And – we've been **factual!**

We were **ambitious** and, for the first time ever, **successful!**

I cannot **tell** you how **happy** it makes me feel ... driving a **proper** Ferrari again.

Ferrari 430 Scuderia

Engine: 4.3 litre V8

Power: 510bhp

0-60mph: 3.1 seconds

Max. speed: 198mph

TG Track time: 1min 19.7secs

Good stuff:

- Loads and loads of very geeky tweaks to make it go scarily fast including a lot of computers that allow it to change gear in 60 milliseconds – faster than you can blink
- Adjustable traction control, stability control and suspension
- Winglets at the front and an undertray at the back maximise downforce – the faster you go, the more grip you have
- Weighs 100kg less than the standard 430, has fatter tyres, and more power
- Partly designed by Michael Schumacher. Whoever he is

Bad stuff:

- No carpets, sat nav, stereo or frills
- Appears to be welded together by apes
- Scuderia is Italian for 'team'. Which is silly
- Costs £172,000 – £43,000 more than the 430
- Tricky to drive fast – a technical racer

Listen... **listen** to the noise. You only have to **flex** your big toe.

Whoops! Oh dear, that has **not** gone well.

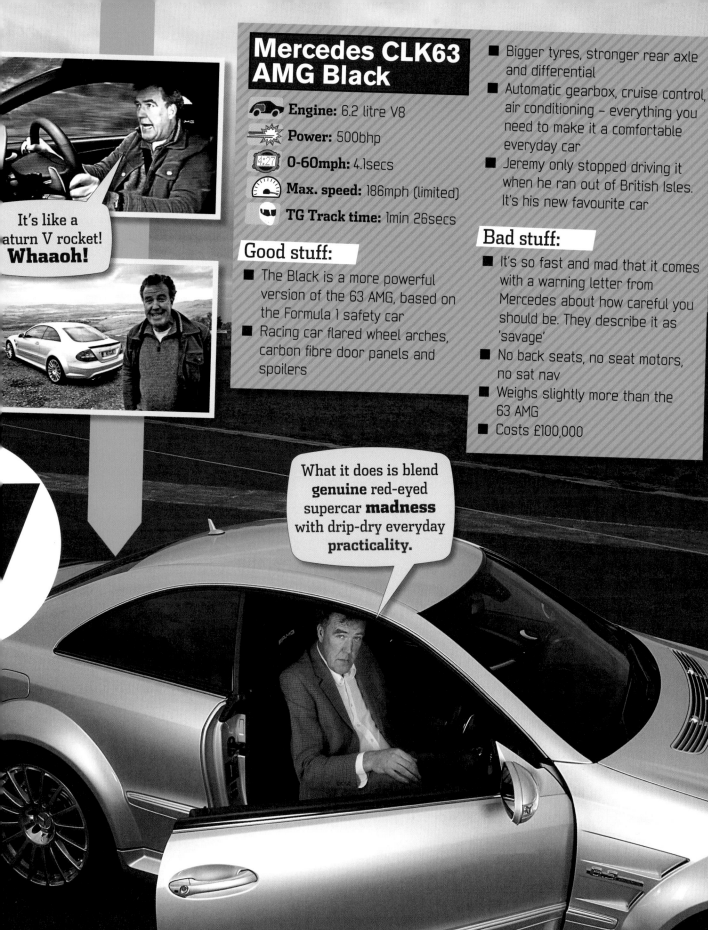

It's like a Saturn V rocket! **Whaaoh!**

Mercedes CLK63 AMG Black

Engine: 6.2 litre V8

Power: 500bhp

0-60mph: 4.1secs

Max. speed: 186mph (limited)

TG Track time: 1min 26secs

Good stuff:

- The Black is a more powerful version of the 63 AMG, based on the Formula 1 safety car
- Racing car flared wheel arches, carbon fibre door panels and spoilers
- Bigger tyres, stronger rear axle and differential
- Automatic gearbox, cruise control, air conditioning – everything you need to make it a comfortable everyday car
- Jeremy only stopped driving it when he ran out of British Isles. It's his new favourite car

Bad stuff:

- It's so fast and mad that it comes with a warning letter from Mercedes about how careful you should be. They describe it as 'savage'
- No back seats, no seat motors, no sat nav
- Weighs slightly more than the 63 AMG
- Costs £100,000

What it does is blend **genuine** red-eyed supercar **madness** with drip-dry everyday **practicality.**

BEAT THE BUNKERS

Can you find out which of these clunking relics from the Cold War actually makes it through the bunkers, banks and barriers of this old missile base?

Oh dear, I've **accidentally** killed James May there...

I've gone – there's **nothing** I can do!

F1 Speed Merchants

Five F1 greats have risked their hard-won reputation racing round our race track in a Reasonably Priced Car. Can you match up each driver with their correct time? And did any of them manage to beat our tame racing driver?

Lewis Hamilton (wet & oily)

Nigel Mansell

Jenson Button (hot)

Mark Webber (very wet)

Damon Hill

1 min 44.6 secs

1 min 44.7 secs

1 min 44.7 secs

1 min 46.3 secs

1 min 47.1 secs

The One Tank Challenge

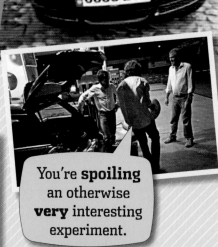

The Top Gear team was asked to switch on Blackpool's famous illuminations but of course, it only takes one person to flick a switch. So, to find 'the chosen one', the producers came up with a race, from Basel in Switzerland all the way to Blackpool. That's 750 miles... on just ONE tank of petrol!

> You're **spoiling** an otherwise **very** interesting experiment.

> If you're going to **fail**, you may as well fail in **style** and **comfort.**

Basel town centre – the night before the race

James turned up in a Subaru Legacy, which he'd chosen because it had a huge fuel tank – a useful accessory in this challenge.

Jeremy had gone for a completely unsuitable Jaguar XJ6 and you sensed that he wasn't really taking things seriously!

As for Richard, he'd plumped for a VW Polo BlueMotion, an eco car that, he claimed, would do a whopping 74 miles to the gallon.

However, what they all soon realised was that on paper, none of their cars could actually do the necessary 750 miles on one tank of petrol. The challenge looked doomed to fail before they'd even started!

A Swiss petrol station – very early next morning

The lads were preparing. Richard checked his tyre pressures, James made his car more aerodynamic with some hi-tech sticky tape and Jeremy had a cup of coffee.

In an attempt to slow James down, Richard and Jezza had filled his boot with what can only be described as 'lots of heavy things'!

The start

Richard had chosen the shortest route, although it did go through the mountains, while James went for a longer route that was flatter. As for Jeremy, he just blasted along the motorways, which made his journey over 80 miles longer. He hoped that would mean he dropped out first!

On a French motorway

Jeremy was now putting his foot down, as well as turning on every gizmo he had to try and make the Jag even less fuel efficient.

Meanwhile, the dullest duel in motoring history was unfolding, as Richard and James played cat and mouse. Neither of them wanted to use up vital fuel by putting their foot down!

> I had worked out that if I went **fast** enough I would conk out on the M40, just a few minutes from **my house.**

> I'm **desperate** for a pee!

> It's **neck and neck,** ladies and gentlemen!

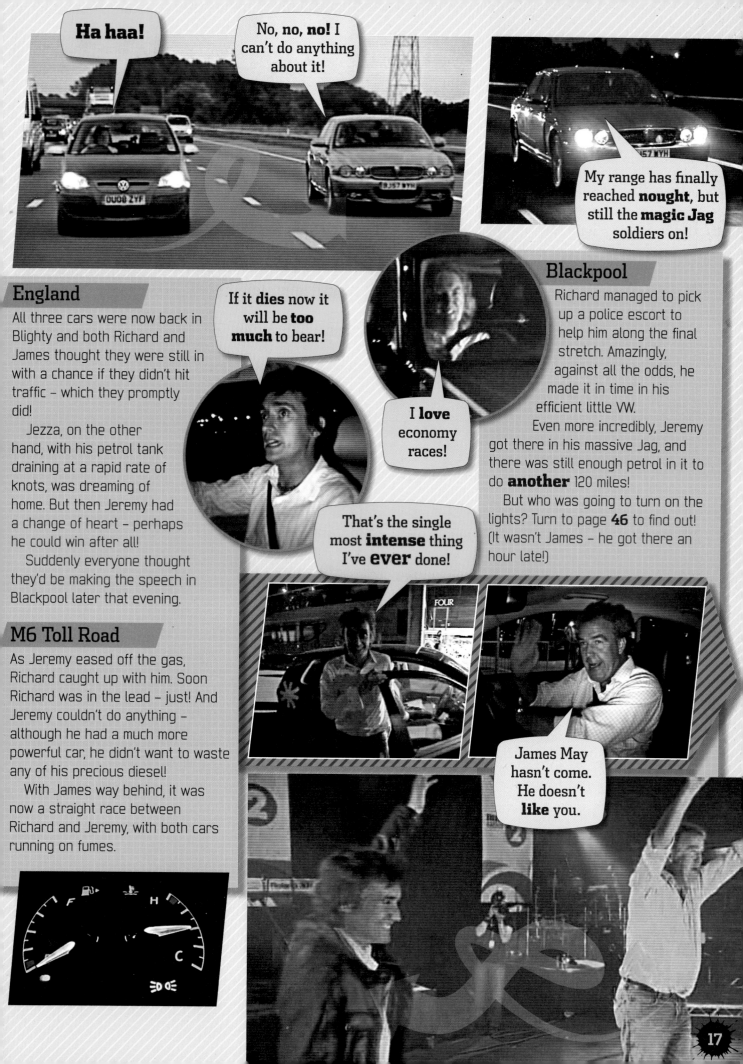

Ha haa!

No, no, **no!** I can't do anything about it!

My range has finally reached **nought**, but still the **magic Jag** soldiers on!

England

All three cars were now back in Blighty and both Richard and James thought they were still in with a chance if they didn't hit traffic – which they promptly did!

Jezza, on the other hand, with his petrol tank draining at a rapid rate of knots, was dreaming of home. But then Jeremy had a change of heart – perhaps he could win after all!

Suddenly everyone thought they'd be making the speech in Blackpool later that evening.

If it **dies** now it will be **too much** to bear!

I **love** economy races!

M6 Toll Road

As Jeremy eased off the gas, Richard caught up with him. Soon Richard was in the lead – just! And Jeremy couldn't do anything – although he had a much more powerful car, he didn't want to waste any of his precious diesel!

With James way behind, it was now a straight race between Richard and Jeremy, with both cars running on fumes.

Blackpool

Richard managed to pick up a police escort to help him along the final stretch. Amazingly, against all the odds, he made it in time in his efficient little VW.

Even more incredibly, Jeremy got there in his massive Jag, and there was still enough petrol in it to do **another** 120 miles!

But who was going to turn on the lights? Turn to page **46** to find out! (It wasn't James – he got there an hour late!)

That's the single most **intense** thing I've **ever** done!

James May hasn't come. He doesn't **like** you.

We Brits have made some fantastic cars* over the years, and been pretty darn good at driving them too. Hurrah!

Twelve of the Best

Can you find these twelve famous motoring names in the grid below? These great names really do represent Britain at its very best – cue a fanfare, play the national anthem and shout out loud – Blighty, we love you! (OK, we admit it, Rovers were a bit rubbish in the end, but you can't win them all!)

TVR	Jaguar	Rolls Royce	Daimler
Aston Martin	Mini	Lotus	Caterham
Morgan	Triumph	Bentley	Rover

R	E	L	M	I	A	D	M	I	N	S	A	G
O	S	T	O	R	L	A	R	T	L	E	J	T
V	M	U	G	T	O	I	T	B	E	A	M	J
R	A	I	M	D	U	M	V	R	G	S	T	A
E	S	R	O	L	L	S	R	O	Y	C	E	G
M	T	A	R	E	B	D	A	I	M	R	L	U
R	O	R	G	A	H	E	R	T	A	C	E	A
G	N	T	A	R	T	V	N	U	A	R	Y	R
A	M	I	N	I	U	I	R	T	P	O	H	V
N	A	N	U	A	R	G	E	S	L	V	T	L
T	R	O	G	U	A	R	G	A	J	E	N	R
L	T	T	A	R	H	A	M	C	T	R	Y	H
E	I	S	J	A	H	P	M	U	I	R	T	A
Y	N	A	M	O	G	R	A	N	I	T	A	M

World Land Speed Record

Challenging for the World Land Speed Record is all about guts and commitment. And speed.

The race to find the fastest thing on wheels began in quite a sedate fashion, with the French and Belgians dominating the early years of the competition. The wonderfully named Gaston de Chasseloup-Laubat set the first ever mark in 1898 – a rather tame 39.24 mph!

Things began to hot up after the First World War and in 1924, Malcolm Campbell, driving Bluebird ⊙, took

the record with a time of 146.15 on Pendine Sands in Wales.

Three years later fellow Brit Henry Seagrave became the first person over 200 mph in his car Sunbeam ⊙, but then in 1935 Campbell hit back, becoming the first man to blast along at over 300 mph. The rest of the world could only sit back and watch in amazement!

* And a few duffers, to be honest

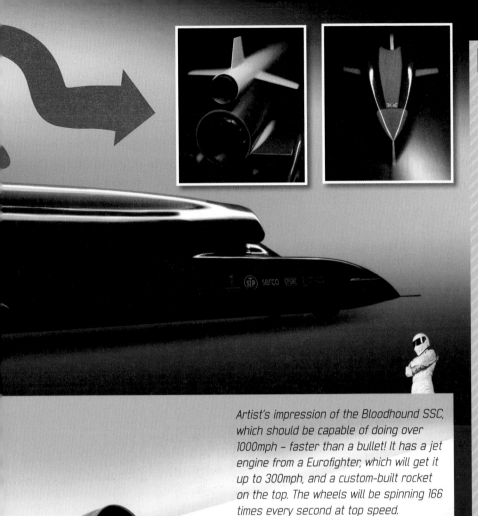

Of course, it's not all been good! Here are four British cars that we should probably all just forget about. Strange, but they all seem to have been built in the 1970s - the decade that style forgot!

Austin Allegro – it started to go rusty if you even mentioned the word rain. And it also had an awful square steering wheel.

Morris Ital – the Italian design team on this one must have been having a bad day at the office when they came up with this monstrosity!

Morris Marina – a British attempt to take on the mighty Ford Cortina that was doomed to failure. Far too many were a sludgy brown colour, too.

Artist's impression of the Bloodhound SSC, which should be capable of doing over 1000mph – faster than a bullet! It has a jet engine from a Eurofighter, which will get it up to 300mph, and a custom-built rocket on the top. The wheels will be spinning 166 times every second at top speed.

In 1948 Englishman John Cobb ⊖ set another record, at over 392 mph, but this was to be the last one set in a 'normal' car. The Americans decided to move the goalposts, and began a new era of jet-propelled cars. It took us a bit of time to catch up, but catch up we did!

In 1983 Richard Noble ⊖ topped 633mph in his car Thrust 2 ⊘ and

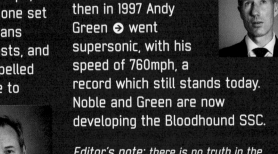

then in 1997 Andy Green ⊖ went supersonic, with his speed of 760mph, a record which still stands today. Noble and Green are now developing the Bloodhound SSC.

Editor's note: there is no truth in the rumour that James May has been asked to attempt to break the record in the Bloodhound SSC. Absolutely no truth at all!

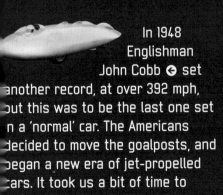

Triumph TR7 – horrible wedge of a car, that was meant to be futuristic but turned out to be a sports car without much power. It was given the code name Bullet during its design, which is basically what it got after sales failed to take off.

SAVE OUR CARAVANS!

WE INTERRUPT THIS ANNUAL FOR A PUBLIC SERVICE ANNOUNCEMENT FROM THE NCPCC, THE NATIONAL CAMPAIGN FOR THE PREVENTION OF CRUELTY TO CARAVANS.

There are over half a million caravans in Britain. They come in all shapes and sizes, with something to suit almost anybody. They are reliable and dependable (though not very attractive), and if looked after properly can live for a very long time. Almost all of them are loved and cared for by their owners.

Sadly, some caravans fall into the wrong hands. These poor things suffer terribly at the hands of twisted bullies that get pleasure out of hurting these poor, defenceless creatures. Some of their methods are very inventive and original, quite funny even...

No! No! It's wrong. Stop it! Just look at the horrible things that can happen to caravans!

SPEEDING!

A long-haired layabout towed a defenceless caravan at 124.9mph behind a Mitsubishi Evo VII. This is much faster than the legal towing speed of 50mph. The caravan got badly shaken and even lost the kitchenette window.

DROPPING!

Not satisfied with that, the heartless layabout strung the caravan up by its tow hitch and dropped it onto some really hard concrete. There wasn't much left after that.

CRRUMMP

BURNING!

A short hooligan parked a perfectly good Monza caravan behind a massively powerful dragster (0-200mph in 3.8secs, 100 gallons to the mile). When the dragster's jet engine was fired up, the poor caravan was badly blistered. Really very badly.

JUMPING!

As if that wasn't enough, the wee fella then crushed some defenceless caravans under a ridiculous stretch limousine that weighed THREE TONS. Come on, is that really fair?

DARTS!

Things got really sick when the short one and the long-haired one got together. They egged each other on in a horrible game: throwing cars at a sweet little caravan to see which of them could hit it. The short one could. Awwww.

REPLAY

CONKERS!

The gruesome twosome tried another game with six caravans – conkers. They forced the lickle caravans to bash into each other, over and over again, until bits fell off. Or they broke.

CHIP FRYING!

The little one and the hairy one went on a proper caravan holiday with their mate, a big bully. The idea was for them to finally experience the joys of caravanning, so they'd stop being so cruel. Sadly, the big bully set fire to their caravan when he tried to cook chips in the fully-equipped proper kitchen. Which didn't have a fire extinguisher.

MORE JUMPING!

The hairy one and a spotty teenager threw two more remote-controlled cars at a cuddly Senator caravan. Sadly, it didn't survive. Hardly surprising really.

TOWING!

The short one wasn't even driving when his car went past a Demolition Ball of Death towing a caravan; he was using remote control. The damage is still all his fault though.

FLYING!

This was just the height of madness. Caravans are fantastically versatile, but they were never meant to fly.

If you care about caravans, support the work of the National Campaign for the Prevention of Cruelty to Caravans. And stop watching these three horrid men hurting the poor things. Please?

21

James' Roller V Jeremy's Merc

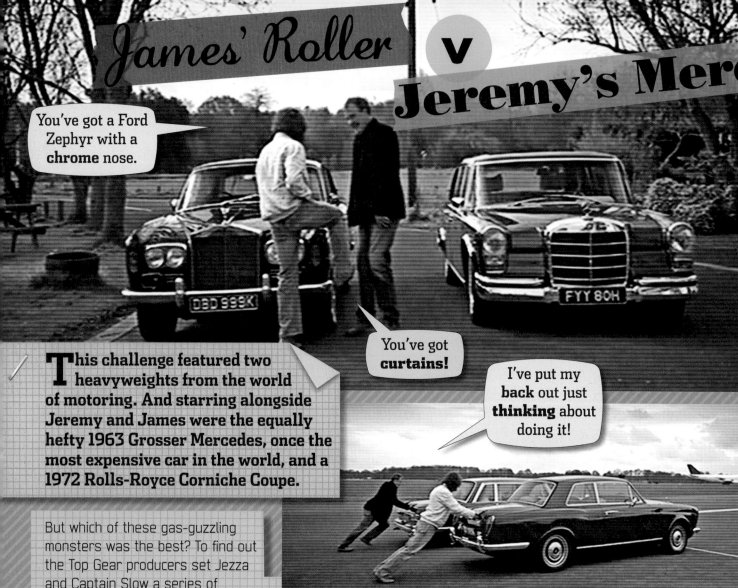

You've got a Ford Zephyr with a **chrome** nose.

You've got **curtains!**

I've put my **back** out just **thinking** about doing it!

DBD 999K

FYY 80H

This challenge featured two heavyweights from the world of motoring. And starring alongside Jeremy and James were the equally hefty 1963 Grosser Mercedes, once the most expensive car in the world, and a 1972 Rolls-Royce Corniche Coupe.

But which of these gas-guzzling monsters was the best? To find out the Top Gear producers set Jezza and Captain Slow a series of fiendish tests that would stretch their driving – and parking – skills to the max.

The first test was a **slalom** around some cones, which the Stig did in just 24 seconds aboard a nippy little Hyundai.

James then had a go but, let's face it, his Rolls wasn't really built for this sort of a challenge.

So it was left to Jeremy to cruise into the lead, winning by 9 seconds.

Next up was a quarter mile **drag race** – without engines. Yep, it was all down to the pushing power of our super-fit presenters.

Because old cars break down a lot, reasoned the producers, owners had to get used to pushing them out of harm's way.

They struggled to budge the cars – not surprising given that both beasts weighed in at over two tonnes. Eventually, James managed to shift his a couple of centimetres. Jeremy just collapsed and James claimed victory.

For the next test, Jeremy and James were actually allowed to start their engines, as this time the producers wanted to see which of these luxury cruisers could go the **fastest**.

James went first, got it up to 97 mph but couldn't stop – and ended up skidding off into the grass.

I'm going to be **sick!**

RRMMMBL

As ever, Jeremy was supremely confident and he managed to coax his car through the 100 mph barrier, but he too found stopping a bit more tricky!

Finally, the duo headed for London to **park** their cars. What could be simpler? This, said James, was the easiest challenge in the history of Top Gear. Oh really?

My brakes are **on fire!**

In London our cars were plainly **so** much better than anyone else's.

When the Mercedes and the Rolls ruled the road, there wasn't half as much traffic around. Today though, the roads are chock-a-block full of neat little hatchbacks, not cars the size of buses.

Jeremy, who once used to live in London, was confident he could reverse into a space. But it all went horribly wrong and he ended up blocking the road. His car was just too big.

God, this is embarrassing.

When they did eventually find a parking space they couldn't work the ticket machine!

In the end they headed for a good old multi-storey car park. Jeremy soon found a space and parked perfectly... the only trouble was, he couldn't get out of his massive car!

They were then thrown out after Jeremy sounded his ultra-loud horn.

As they continued their search, James' Roller decided to run out of petrol and Captain Slow was forced to siphon some out of the Mercedes.

Eventually they decided enough was enough but Jeremy still managed to claim victory because not only could you fit more petrol in his Mercedes but it also had a much louder horn.

Once again, a very scientific conclusion to a Top Gear Challenge!

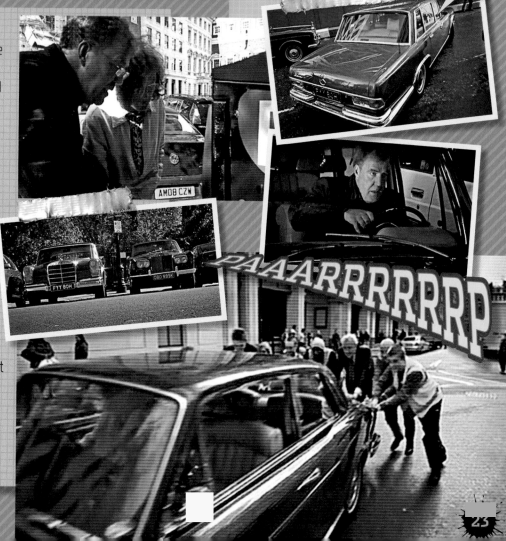

PAAARRRRRRP

Police Car Challenge!

Will a second-hand car be any good as a police car? Play this board game to find out – and see if you can catch that crim!

The Rules

1. Throw a 6 to see who goes first.
2. Use coins or counters and take turns to move around the board. If you land on a space with an instruction on it, you must do as it says.
3. You've got to throw the exact number to win the game.
4. Strictly no cheating, or you're NICKED!

START

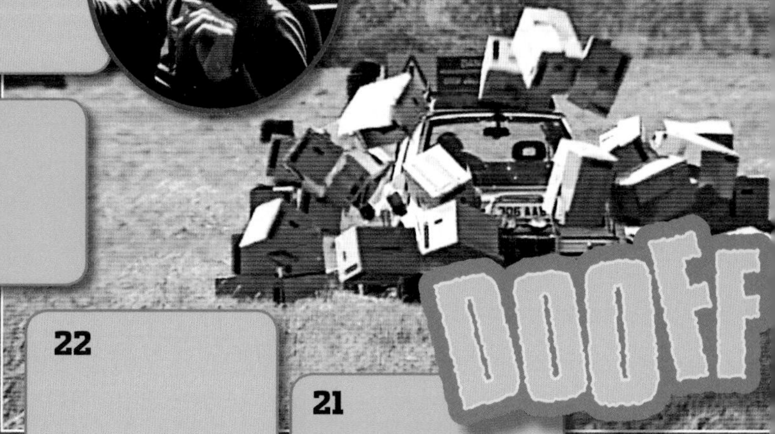

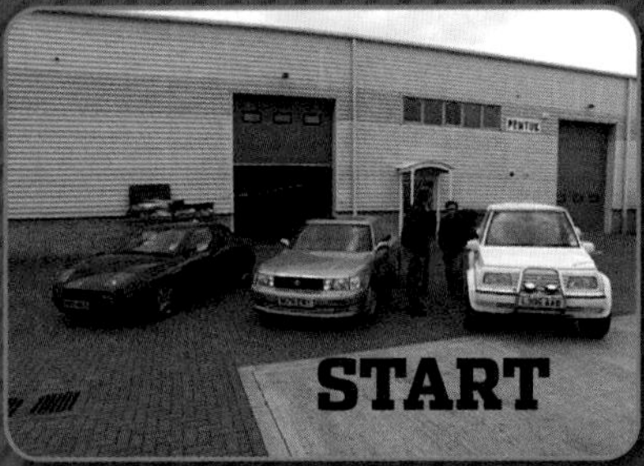

1

2

3 *With 500 quid, turn your clapped-out motor into the perfect police car. **Move on 3 spaces.***

4

5

6

7 *Try and beat the St who's doing a lap in* **real** *police car. Tho again!*

It's Officer **Barbie!**

20

21 *Show off your stylish driving skills and plough through a load of boxes. **Move on 6 spaces!***

22

23

24

25 *Stop to help sort out the scene of an accident. **Miss a turn!***

26

27

28

29

30

That looked **good** in slow motion!

DOOFF

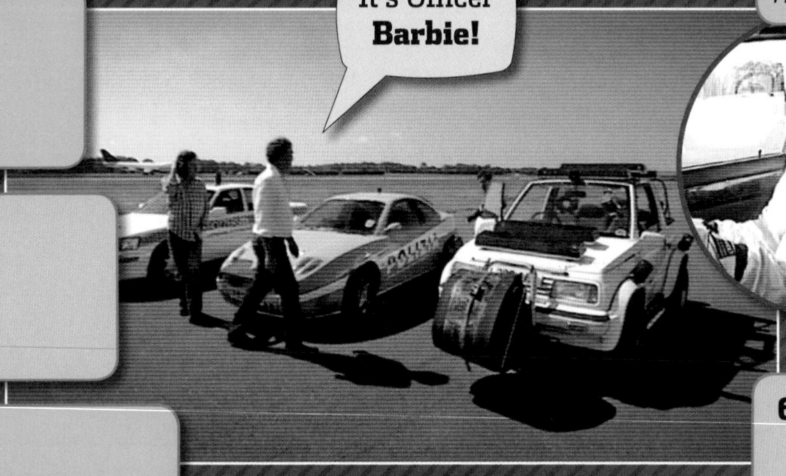

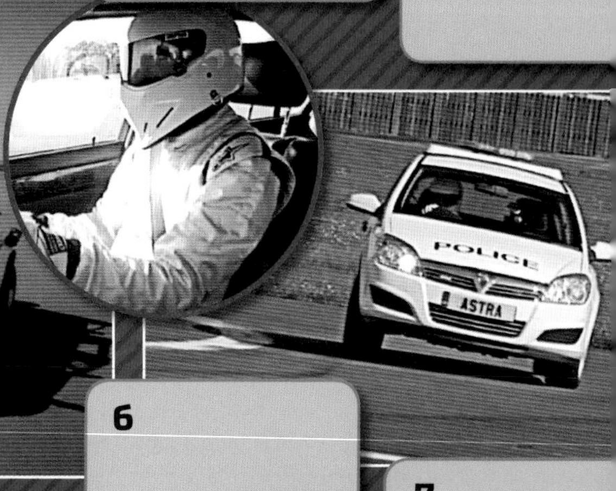

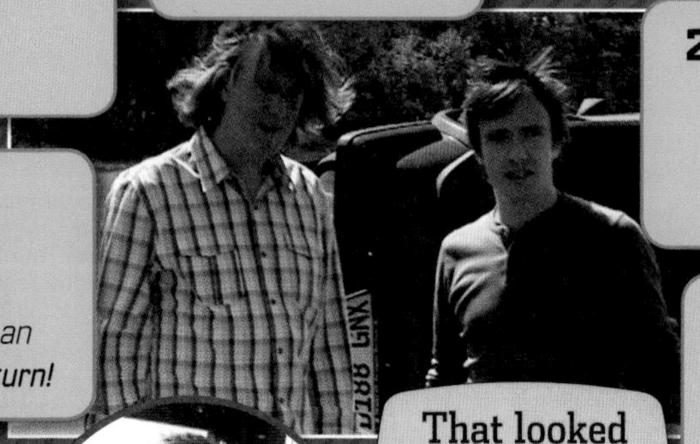

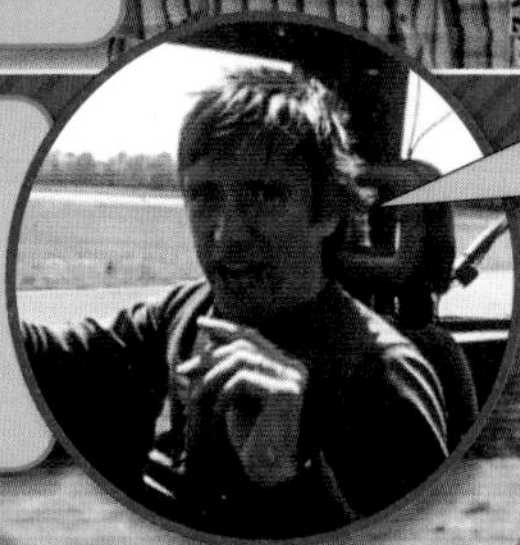

1min 53.4secs

1min 51.7secs

Rob Brydon and James Corden

Actors (and James is a co-writer) from Gavin & Stacey

How was it?

Rob was relaxed about the day, and I'll tell you why: he'd done it before, *and* beaten his mate Steve Coogan. However that didn't stop him spinning off on his first practice lap. And the second. And all the others. James thought it was good... although he'd **never** driven a manual car before.

Car history

When James took his driving test, he already had *nine* points on his provisional licence, thanks to some dangerous antics on his moped. He only ever passed the automatic test!

Justin Lee Collins & Alan Carr

Comedians and presenters of The Sunday Night Project

How was it?

For Alan the day went smoothly. Justin spun off twice during his practice laps (that second-to-last bend is a sneaky one). Stig was very nice to him: 'It's Nigel Havers.'

Car history

Justin's got a Honda Civic, bought on the basis of what James May said: 'He's got long hair and he's from Bristol. You can't go wrong.'

Get in gear! First, fifth, that's third... **Who** drives a manual? **No-one!**

Peter Firth and Rupert Penry-Jones

Actors from Spooks

How was it?

Rupert went off spectacularly on the second-to-last corner in practice. He had to get out of the passenger door because he dented the driver's side. And then he went off-road in his timed lap!

Car history

Peter once left a 1966 Mercedes in a car park for two years. When he finally remembered it, he didn't have the £5000 parking fees – so they took the car. Ouch.

Terrifying. Really scary. You're going very fast.

1min 51.2secs

1min 51.2secs

I kept doing that 'mirror, signal manoeuvre' and then I realised there were no other **cars.**

Fiona Bruce and Kate Silverton

Newsreaders and presenters

How was it?

Kate was very good, according to the Stig. He thought Fiona was the most stubborn: 'I don't like being told what to do.'

Car history

Fiona is fond of her mumvan – a Citroen C4 Picasso. 'I love it, it does everything for you.' Jeremy wasn't particularly jealous: 'It's a hateful car!'

> **BEEP** Sorry! I don't know why I'm apologising for **swearing**, but I'm a newsreader...

> **So** much more fun than the school run!

1min 57.4secs

1min 54.7secs

1min 47.1secs

> Come on **come on**! This has got **nothing**!

> We're both **knackered**. It's **very** hard. You have to concentrate for so long.

1min 48.1secs

Theo Paphitis and Peter Jones

Businessmen and Dragons' Den judges

How was it?

This pair of very competitive petrolheads enjoyed themselves enormously. Theo almost lost it on Gambon – the Stig was scared, and shouted at him. However Stiggy was impressed by Peter.

Car history

They both have Maybachs, costing over £300,000. Jeremy felt they could do better: 'Unwise, gentlemen. Very, very unwise.'

> There'll be **no clutch left** in this car by the time I've finished!

1min 48.5secs

The Fastest Star!

1min 46.9secs

Bullet Train v Nissan GTR

Japan – a country that loves things that are super-sleek and super-fast. Two of their finest inventions are the 200 mph Bullet Train and the 193 mph Nissan GTR. But which is best?

Hakui-Shi

Kyoto

Tokyo

Finish

Jeremy jumped behind the wheel of the GTR, while James and Richard went for the train option in a race from one side of Japan to the other, with the first to reach a statue of a Buddha dedicated to road safety declared the winner.

So would Japan's legendary traffic jams be the undoing of Jeremy, or would Richard and James simply get lost as they tried to catch four trains, a bus, a ferry and a cable car – which also meant their journey was 150 miles longer.

As ever, Jeremy was confident of victory.

> A **boy** from Birmingham and a man with **no** sense of direction **in Japan** won't win – **the end.**

> ‹Is-this-seat-taken?›

> Hang on, **that's** not right.

Working out the language was proving tricky. They had all been given translation machines to help them but they only seemed to add to the confusion!

Jeremy had a sat nav, which was crucial since he didn't understand any of the roadsigns. However he was terrified of touching it, in case he accidentally turned it off.

When 'Amy' started giving him instructions in Japanese, he got a bit worried.

> HELP!

I've seen X Factor winners **less cheerful** than **all** the petrol pump attendants in Japan.

Jeremy was now so confident of winning that even when he did have to stop at traffic lights, he just saw it as a chance to play with some of the toys the office had provided.

GA-DANNG

Jeremy was edging in front but still had to stop off for petrol.

But he was soon back on the road, and it was Jeremy who got to Tokyo first. "Tokyo is where the battle will be won or lost," said James, which was rather stating the obvious, seeing as that's where the finish line was.

It's about fifty miles from one side of the city to the other and James was convinced that Jezza was heading straight into the jaws of one of Tokyo's legendary traffic jams. But incredibly the roads were almost completely clear.

But then he began fiddling with Amy, his sat nav, and disaster struck!

BIP

Oh my **god**, I've just turned the **sat nav** off.

And with all the instructions in Japanese, he was struggling to turn it back on again.

This was a great chance for the others to take the lead, but somehow they managed to muck things up by getting on different trains!

Something **peculiar** has happened – we're not on the **same train.**

Tokyo's not a **city**, it's a **race track!**

Back in the GTR...

Amy's back on my screen – I pushed everything and she's back!

Richard and James were now reunited on the bus taking them to the ferry and soon everyone was crossing the bay, with Jeremy hurtling underneath it, and the others sailing peacefully across it.

The ferry docked a mile from the cable car so it was out with the fold-up bikes for Richard and James.

Jeremy's sat nav told him that he was going to arrive six minutes after the others, so he put the GTR into race mode.

The others had now dumped their bikes and jumped on the cable car.

It would all be down to a final charge up a mountain and Jeremy was confident this was where the GTR would really come alive.

Both teams were now converging on the Buddha from two different directions. But was Jeremy fit enough to make it up the last flight of steps in time?

Incredibly he was! He edged it by just over three minutes.

This is so damn close!

They aren't here! I've just beaten the bullet train!

Genuinely, honestly? Three minutes twelve seconds!

How long have you been here?

I'm... disappointed!

The Super Quiz

Welcome to this year's fiendishly difficult super quiz. You can have two points for every one you get right, but for every question you get wrong, your best mate can give you a Chinese burn. Still up for the challenge? Excellent, well try this one for starters...

1 Which car gave Jeremy a real pain in the neck?
- a Nissan GTR
- b Gumpert Apollo
- c Audi RS6

2 'I do believe that on this track, old Quasimodo here can destroy every other supercar alive.' Which ugly car was Richard talking about?
- a Gumpert Apollo
- b Bugatti Veyron
- c Mercedes McLaren SLR

3 'No big spoilers, no rotating lights; there aren't even any machine guns!' Jeremy found which speedy Italian to be surprisingly sensible?
- a Ferrari 430 Scuderia
- b Fiat 500
- c Lamborghini Gallardo LP560-4

4 'I hope you like prison food, crims,' threatened James during the police car challenge. But in which car did he hope to round up all the local villains?
- a A Bentley
- b A Lexus
- c A Mercedes

5 What did James race to St Tropez in?
- a A car
- b A plane
- c A boat

6 Which of these ingredients didn't make it into the 'smoothie' Jeremy made using a V8 engine?
- a Raw beef and Tabasco sauce
- b James' underpants and a piece of the Stig's big toe nail
- c A brick and some chillies

7 What did Jeremy use to demonstrate the size of the boot on the new Ford Fiesta?
- a Lots of cheese
- b A stuffed zebra's head
- c Richard wrapped up in cling film

8 What was Toyota's futuristic and nippy 'chair' called?
- a i-ROBOT
- b i-REAL
- c i-RELAX

9 'It has the agility of a flea.' Which nifty little car from Surrey is Richard talking about?
- a Caterham R500
- b Ariel Atom
- c Bentley Brooklands

13 In the Alfa Challenge, Jeremy sprayed his car in what he claimed were Ecuador's racing colours. What colours did he use?

a   Red and green
b   Green and white
c   Orange and silver

0 What was the toilet made out of on the XSR 48 that James piloted to St Tropez?

Carbon fibre
Gold
Wood

14 That 'great' East German car the Trabant was made out of which unlikely material?

a   Woven beetroot stalks
b   Cotton
c   Human hair

1 'Despite weighing over half a ton more, the ****** mullered the Zonda.' What hefty car is James talking about?

Our old friend the Bugatti Veyron
a   a Tesla Roadster
c   a Ford GT

15 When did 'Squadron Leader' May get to fly in a vintage fighter plane?

a   During the Muscle Car challenge
b   During the England v Germany challenge
c   In the Vietnam special

Turn to page 61 for the answers.

12 What did Richard use to recover the seat in his Alfa Romeo Spider?

a   Jeremy's leather jacket
b   A black bin bag
c   The Stig's driving leathers

Scoring

26+ points
You're the accelerator pedal!
You're the real thing, the power behind everything. Congratulations.

16-25 points
You're the spark plugs!
Well done. You bring life to the party but there's still room for improvement.

11-15 points
You're an exhaust pipe!
OK, so you've got a role to play, but you're full of hot air. And you dribble occasionally.

0-10 points
You're a spare tyre!
Once in a while you come in handy but you obviously spend most of your time shut up in the dark. You need to get out more.

Modding Madness

A Mitsubishi Evolution X costs £30,000. Could the chaps spend half that amount modifying a second-hand car and make it as fast as the Evo? In two days? Err...

Jeremy, Richard and James were given one of the extremely rare cars that they all liked*. Their target was the Evo's lap time: 1min 28.2secs. Their Renault Avantime could only manage 1min 42.5secs.

New brakes, bigger wheels and tyres saved them precisely... no time at all.

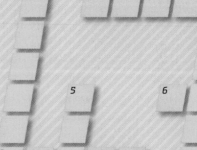

Richard donated an old Formula One rear spoiler, which made it even slower.

Jeremy insisted a splitter would help, but they could only afford a wooden one and it caught fire.

Overnight, James got to fiddle with the engine to get more POWER. It didn't help much. His view? Modding is pointless!

Evo 10 Time   1.28.2
Best Lap Time 1.36.2   1.37.0

ACROSS

3) What round things did they end up buying eight of?
6) This Formula One plank on the back didn't help.
8) Their car had a lot of this.
10) Which Japanese speed-demons make the Evo?
11) Who thought a bit of wood screwed to the front would help?
12) And what did he cut it out with?

DOWN

1) Complete the phrase had Jeremy always wanted to say: 'And now, back to the...'
2) James loves fiddling with engines, but Jeremy and Richard think it's...
4) They're complicated springs that make a car bounce in the right way.
5) The make of French boxy car they had to modify.
7) Car maker with a logo like a fat diamond.
9) What potato-based fuel kept James going through the night?

*Along with the Ford Mondeo and Subaru Legacy, fact fans.

Car-Doku!

How to play

The grid shows nine 'garages' of nine squares each. Every row, column and garage has to contain exactly one car of each colour (and there are nine colours, if you can't count). Work out what colour car the empty spaces have to contain. Use coloured pens to fill in the grid, or cut out these counters and place them on the grid to solve it.

Boring old Sudoku with numbers has been keeping commuters quiet for ages, but finally there's a version for people who like cars. Hooray!

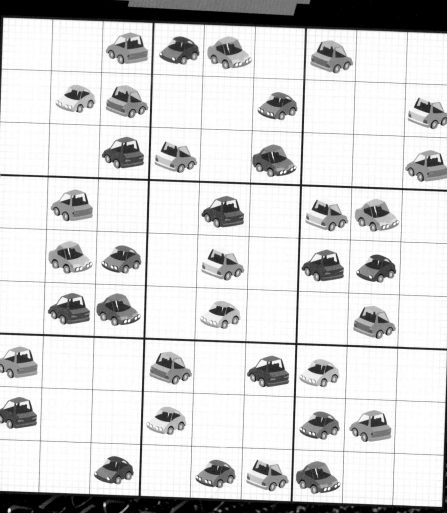

35

Mitsuoka Orochi

 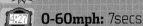

- **Engine:** 3.3 litre V6
- **Power:** 231bhp
- **0-60mph:** 7secs
- **Max. speed:** Captain Slow never got a chance to find out in Tokyo, but probably around 150mph

Good stuff:

The styling is based on a fish, a snake and Pamela Anderson's mouth... apparently
Named after an 8-headed dragon
Only costs £44,000
Hand-built to order, with 200 paint colour choices and 25 trim options
5-speed automatic – easy to drive
Quiet, comfortable and with an excellent ride

> The ride is actually rather **excellent**, for a supercar. So obviously, I think it suits me **rather well**.

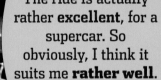

Bad stuff:

Some of the interior is artificial leather and metal-plated plastic, to save cost
Some parts are borrowed from cheaper cars
Not very fast for a sportscar
Who the heck are Mitsuoka? No-one's heard of them
Those looks. You either love them or...

Mitsuoka Galue

- **Engine:** 3.5litre V6
- **Power:** 155bhp
- **0-60mph:** don't know
- **Top speed:** look, it's not that kind of car

Good stuff:

- Could be Japan's Rolls-Royce
- Only costs a wallet-friendly £32,000
- Wood-ish interior, plush leather upholstery
- Sat nav and air conditioning
- It made James smile

Bad stuff:

- An 'utterly shameless rip-off' of a British luxury car
- Jerky to drive, swampy cornering – very much *not* like a Roller
- Feels like a cheap version of an expensive watch
- The satnav only talks Japanese
- Not comfy enough for sumo wrestlers

> It's **not** taking itself **too** seriously. It's just a bit of **fun.**

Muddy Mayhem

You can't mess about on the roads. It's not safe, it's too crowded and they won't let you. However, if you've got a big field and Santa's been generous, you can have *quite a lot* of fun going off-road.

VRRRAAAAAHHH

Racing quads

The quad bike is very popular, because it's reliable and practical. But for some people, they aren't quite *fun* enough. What the quad needs, in their opinion, is a really BIG engine. To turn it into a racing quad.

These come in a thousand flavours, so which one would the chaps like best? Time for a play in the mud.

Jeremy had a few problems getting his two-wheel drive Yamaha 450 racer started. When he finally worked out what gear he was in, he took it up to the top speed of one million miles an hour. But he was a *bit* scared.

Richard meanwhile tried a Honda, with a single-cylinder 450cc engine producing a thousand million horsepower. It goes faster than light. Honest.

After a bit of practice, they learned to enjoy getting dirty at high speed. But they didn't think these muddy, scary quads were quite James's cup of tea.

I'm too **tall**, and I'm too **old**, and I'm too **fat**, and I **hate it.**

VRUMM

I'd never, **ever** tell Jeremy, but... I'm **terrified!**

I'd give the **rest** of my year's salary to see that **sink.**

ArgoCat

If a quad bike's four wheels seem a little inadequate or unsafe, there is an alternative: the ArgoCat , which has eight. It costs £12,000, and only gets up to 22mph. But it's rugged, can spin on the spot and doesn't stop for anything – even water.

Qpod

They were right. James was trying out the very sensible Qpod sport. For £5,000 it has seatbelts, comfy chairs (handy because James had recently had an operation on his bum), a 340cc single-cylinder engine, and steers like a scooter. Plus it can do something the quads can't.

> Here's what I like best... it's **completely** road-legal. You need **never, ever** drive it off-road. Oh joy!

> The speed is just... **Whoah!** I'm in a **fighter jet!**

Buggies

The top level on the off-road fun-o-meter is taken by buggies. They're beautifully simple: four wheels, some scaffolding, a seat and an engine. What more do you need?

Richard was blown away by the £12,500 Drakart. Powered by a 600cc snowmobile engine, it can do 0-60mph in under 3 seconds and reach 110mph. Which is a lot when your backside is an inch above a cowpat.

Jeremy's Rage buggy costs about the same as the Drakart, and looks similar. But it has a 900cc engine from a Honda Fireblade (that's a motorbike). It gets to 60mph faster than a Ferrari Enzo.

Jeremy and Richard agreed the buggies were loads more fun than the quads (and more comfortable).

BA-**DOOM**

> I've been killed. I've **definitely** been killed.

Hovercrafts

James thought they were a pair of yobs. In a single day, Jeremy and Richard had completely chewed up all the grass. But Jeremy had the solution: a hovercraft. You build it yourself from a kit, for about £6,000. The handling is a bit rubbish, they're very noisy, but the fun levels are off the scale.

Jeremy still managed to damage the field a bit... by crashing. And dying.

MINE'S BIGGER THAN YOURS

> Over the **years** this track has claimed more than **200** lives.

Which would you rather drive round: the Top Gear Track, or the Nürburgring? Time to decide!

The Top Gear track was designed to test a car's overall quality. Top speed and acceleration are not the most important things here – roadholding, power, weight, balance, suspension, brakes and driver ability all count. So the world's fastest production car, the Bugatti Veyron, is not at the top of the Power Board.

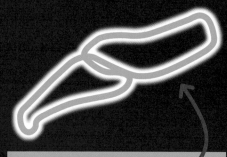

Top Gear Track

Location: Dunsfold Park, an airbase in Surrey

Length: 2.8km (1.75miles) with eight corners

Design: Lotus

Can I have a go? Sorry, no.

Accidents: Plenty – none too serious. There's lots of grass all around for when you spin out of control. The cars get most of the dings and dents.

Fastest time: The rather terrifying Caparo T1 was taken round in 1min 10.6secs by the Stig – but it can't get over a roadhump, so it doesn't count. The Apollo Gumpert (ugly name, ugly car) tops the Power Board at 1min 17.1secs. Jay Kay is the fastest Star in a Reasonably Priced Car, at 1min 45.83secs.

RRRAAAAARRRR!

Nürburgring

Location: Built in the 1920s around the village and castle of Nürburg, in western Germany

Length: 20.81km (12.93miles) and 73 corners for the main circuit plus 5.15km (3.2miles) and 16 corners for an extra section used in racing competitions

Design: Some very clever German architects

Can I have a go? Yes, but be careful. The Ring is open to the general public most weekends. There are toll gates on the track, where everyone has to slow down, and you pay €21 per lap. It's treated as a one-way normal German road. If you crash, you'll pay for the repairs to the track... and then be fined for dangerous driving.

Trying to time yourself is not a good idea. Still-running stopwatches are often found in crashed cars.

Accidents: Plenty, and nasty ones too. The full track hasn't been used for F1 races since 1976, because emergency vehicles took too long to reach incidents. The track is narrow, hilly and lined with hard metal crash barriers.

Fastest time: In 1975, Niki Lauda in his Ferrari 312 completed a full circuit in 6mins 58.secs – an *average* of 123mph. The fastest road car round the Ring is currently the Dodge Viper, with the Maserati MC12 close behind.

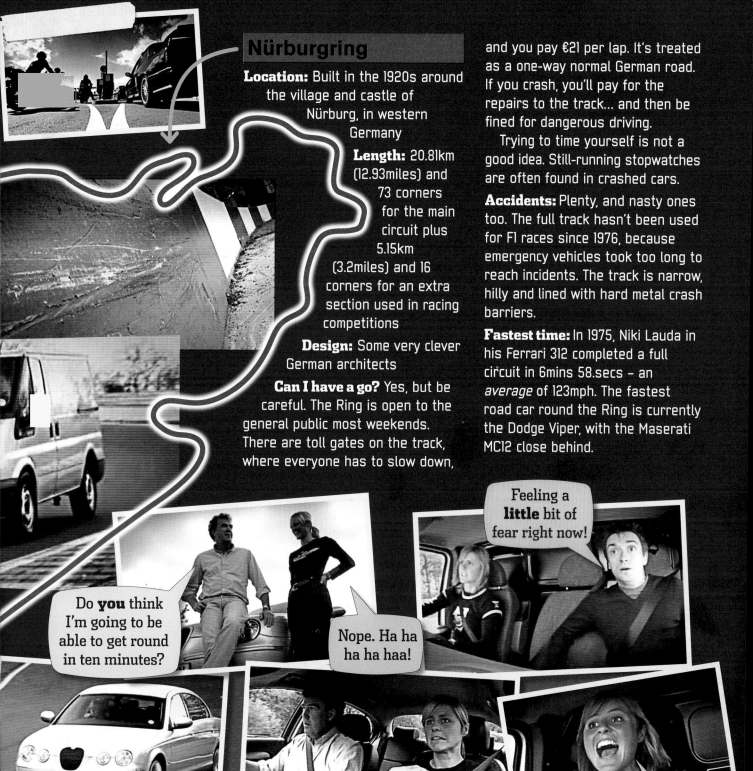

Feeling a **little** bit of fear right now!

Do **you** think I'm going to be able to get round in ten minutes?

Nope. Ha ha ha ha haa!

No please! **Eight** seconds!

The Fastest Taxi Driver in the World

If you don't want to risk your own car round the Ring, take a taxi instead. Pay €180 and three of you can be driven round in a special BMW M5. They're booked a year in advance, but there may be spare seats going, especially when it's wet. The most famous Ring taxi driver is... Sabine Schmitz.

Sabine was brought up in a hotel in Nürburg. She raced for BMW and won the 24 Hour Nürburgring race in 1996 and 1997. These days she teaches advanced driver training and presents a German car show as well as driving the Ring taxi.

She reckons she's lapped the Nürburgring 20,000 times, doing it 1,200 times a year. She helped Jeremy get his diesel Jaguar S-type round the Ring in under ten minutes... just. Then, in the same car, she thrashed his time by 47 seconds! But, despite scaring Richard silly, she couldn't beat his time in a Ford Transit van.

MISTER MAY'S MARVELLOUS MOTORING MOMENTS

> You did it, **you did it!**

J ames May is a sensible, traditional kind of chap. He doesn't like stupid, fiddly over-designed cars and he isn't swayed by power-crazy supercars. And despite his nickname, he is capable of sometimes going fast!

The Scandinavian Flick

During series 12, James found himself in deepest, darkest Finland with another former F1 champ, Mika Hakkinen. He was there to learn the Scandinavian Flick, which isn't a hairstyle but is an expert manoeuvre for cornering at speed during rallying.

The idea was to send the rear of the car in a perfect arch. Using some cones, Mika demonstrated in style, but our James didn't quite get it at first. But then...

> I'm scared already!

> I'll be surprised if you don't turn out to be **better** than the other two.

Slowly, over the day, the lap times gradually began to fall.

Finally James managed to take 20 seconds off his first lap time – success!

> I've passed the BMW! That was a **overtake** on a Finnish person. S[ ] was only **12** but that's not the poin[ ]

Tackling the Tartan Taskmaster

Former motor racing legend Jackie Stewart, one of only a few driving gods to have won the F1 Championships three times, wrote to Top Gear with a challenge. Send any presenter down to the test track, he said, and he'd improve whatever time they registered by a full 20 seconds.

Intrigued, the producers made things even harder for the Tartan Taskmaster by making James his pupil for the day!

James was to attempt the impossible in a TVR Tuscan Convertible. On his first lap he posted a time of 2 mins 26 – the challenge was on.

> Yes, yes, I **knew** it!

> Very good – **good** lap so far – **full power!**

PO55 BKD

Back in the studio...

> I was concentrating so **hard** on learning to drive that I **forgot** I was a TV presenter!

Racing the locals

Having 'mastered' the Finnish art of car control, James entered a bange[ ] race against some locals, most of whom were either OAPs or children!

Despite being forced into a ditch, James called on his new-found Finnish courage and fought back, finishing somewhere near the middle. And that made him exactly average, which he was happy with!

Zonda Zooooomm

With Jeremy and Richard unavailable, and the Top Gear dog at the vets for some worming pills, the producers had no choice but to ask James to road test the raw power of the new Pagani Zonda F.

To give Captain Slow his due, he did try and corner at speed, but just ended up doing a beautifully executed 360 degree spin! Remarkably, he did get better.

In fact he did so well that at one stage it looked like the Stig had lent him his white helmet. Or was it really the Stig wearing James's woolly jumper? We will never know...

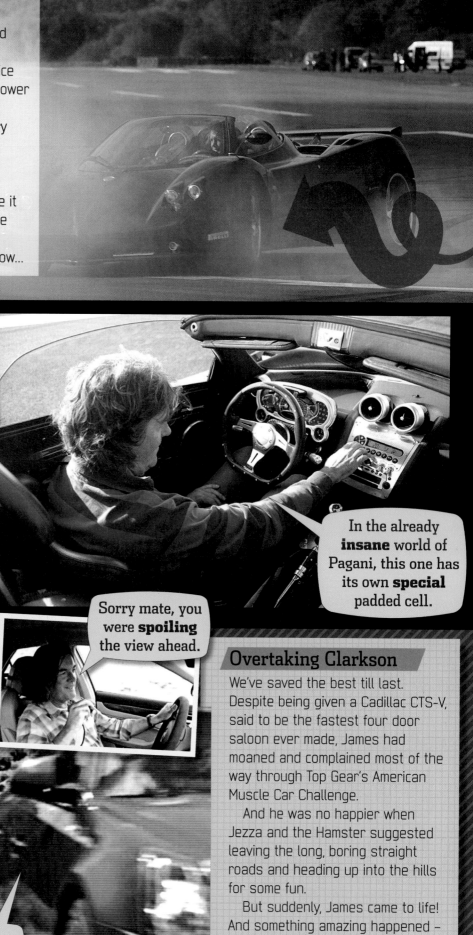

In the already **insane** world of Pagani, this one has its own **special** padded cell.

Sorry mate, you were **spoiling** the view ahead.

Oh my god, **look** at this. I've just been **overtaken!**

What's got in to him?

Try and keep up, Jezza!

Overtaking Clarkson

We've saved the best till last. Despite being given a Cadillac CTS-V, said to be the fastest four door saloon ever made, James had moaned and complained most of the way through Top Gear's American Muscle Car Challenge.

And he was no happier when Jezza and the Hamster suggested leaving the long, boring straight roads and heading up into the hills for some fun.

But suddenly, James came to life! And something amazing happened – James put his foot to the floor and overtook Jeremy and his Corvette!

Germany versus Britain

Which is the greatest motoring nation – Germany, with its Mercedes, BMWs and Porsches or good old GB, with its Aston Martins, Bentleys and Land Rovers?

> We're going to **crush** them and then we can go back **home.**

There was only one way to find out – a series of carefully-crafted challenges between our very own Top Gear team and their counterparts from the D Motor programme in Germany. *Let battle commence!*

The venue was the Zolder Circuit in Belgium, and the Brits arrived in typically flamboyant style, landing in World War II fighter planes!

The Top Gear team were a bit nervous as they were up against some top drivers. The German trio was made up of Sabine Schmitz, also known as the Queen of the Nürburgring, ex-touring car champion Tim Schrick, and a man in a suit called Carsten Van Ryssen.

The first challenge was **Double Decker Racing**, with the Brits mounting Metros on top of Jaguars, while the Germans went for Golfs atop Mercedes. The idea was that the driver in the bottom car controlled the power while the driver at the top had the steering wheel. Cue absolute mayhem!

Unfortunately James and Richard ended up in the gravel, unable to move.

Eventually, the Germans took the points.

The second challenge was a **Drag Race** devised by James. To snuff out the threat of the massive Porsche, the Top Gear team insisted it was only ¼ mile long, which meant the supercar wouldn't have time to get up to top speed!

And it worked, with Richard winning easily in the Ariel Atom.

EEEEEYYYOOOOWWWW

> *James didn't pick the best car for the drag race. Guess where he came?*

> What the **hell** have you done **that** for?

> **This** is our darkest hour.

WWWWWEEEEEEEEEEEEEEEEEEEEEEEEEEEEE

44

Sabine took on Jeremy in the **Mini Cooper Challenge**, which involved a slalom course round some very expensive vases and then a test of reversing skills using a 'garage' full of crockery.

This was followed by a 'J turn' penalty with a huge football (which the Germans missed for once, hooray!), a figure-of-eight skid whilst being shot at by a paintball tank, and then whizzing off through a tunnel of hay bales. Jeremy was utterly useless at all of it!

And then he lost a one lap race of the Zolder track too, pushing the Germans further ahead.

I'm not **talking**, this **matters**.

The fourth challenge saw Richard take on the man in a suit (who didn't even own a car) over a five-lap off-road race in a **Bowler Nemesis**. Surely the Hamster could win this one for the Brits...

Richard was doing well, until he nose-dived off a hill and allowed the German to open up a massive lead.

Incredibly, Richard clawed it back and managed to take the German on the final straight.

The final challenge was a **two-lap race** of the Zolder circuit, which pitted a Porsche against an Aston Martin. The Germans were given a four-second head start.

The Top Gear team claimed that James was driving the Aston, he just happened to have the Stig's white gear on. The Germans weren't quite so sure, especially when the Aston crossed the line first!

Back in the studio James confessed all: "I was bound and gagged in the locker room," and it had in fact been the Stig driving, after all.

But by then the result had been declared – victory for the Brits!

Well done Stig... I mean **James!**

WELCOME TO BLACKPOOL!

Every year a well-known celebrity is invited to turn on the Blackpool Illuminations. Would you be interested? Just look at everything the town has to offer!

Transport links!

The Promenade and Pier

Men with three balls

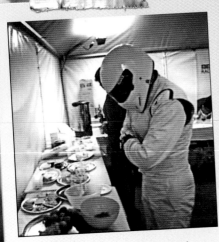

Human food!

Entertainment!

Places to rest!

The Pleasure Beach

Throwing the switch

Machines!*

FZZZZZHH!!

* Payouts are in coins, which can be used to buy things with. In shops.

The Illuminations. Aaah

And — the lights!

47

Cool Wall RIP?

The Cool Wall has suffered over the years since it was unveiled in 2002. Jeremy took a chainsaw to it when Richard tried to put a Ducati motorbike on it. And in the summer of 2007, it got badly burnt in a suspicious fire.* It rose from the ashes in 2008, and Richard and Jeremy had some fun moving things around. But it's all gone quiet recently. Have we seen the last of the Cool Wall?

Fiat Panda moves from Cool to so far below Seriously Uncool it's barely in the studio. Because James May has one.

BMW X6

Ah yes. Cool.

Wrong. This is a truly **shocking** car. It's really uncool and that's an **end** of it.

Jeremy then ripped Richard's mic off so he couldn't argue.

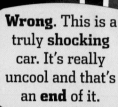
Porsche 911

Peugeot 206 GTi

Audi RS4 is now the new car driven by idiots, so it moves from Cool to Uncool.

Ferrari Enzo

Nissan 350Z

Lotus Exige S

Nissan Micra C+C

It's an expensive **shoe**.

Daihatsu Copen

Jaguar XK

Mercedes SLK55 AMG: Cool (if you're Jeremy) or Uncool (if you're Richard)

You're **not** touching the DB9.

Richard attempted to move all Aston Martins from Sub Zero to Uncool, because too many footballers own them (Wayne Rooney crashed his).

Jezza moved the DB9 up to the top where Richard can't reach it!

It's large and French, so it's **uncool**.

Go on then, I can't be bothered to argue.'

No you're wrong, it's **cool**.

Koenigseggeggseg CCX (the first cool supercar)

Aston Martin DB5

Citroen C5

BMW M3 was Uncool, thanks to the kind of people that liked it. But these drivers have moved on. The only people left driving it these days actually appreciate it. So now it's Cool!

Smart Roadster

Ford StreetKa

Maserati GranSport

Alfa Romeo Brera

Vauxhall Monaro

VW Beetle cabriolet

It's fifteen feet of **car**. Some car. And for the **first time ever**, I can't be bothered to put it on the wall. It is **mild cheddar**.

BMW 3-series

Ford GT was Uncool, until Jeremy decided to buy one, when he moved it to Cool. When he got it, it went to Sub Zero... until he got a bit annoyed by it.

LORRYING: HOW HARD CAN IT BE?

To find out if Jeremy was right, the lads were given £5000 each and told to use their 'extensive knowledge of lorries' (yeah, right!) to buy a second-hand HGV and find out what it's *really* like to be a **lorryist.**

James's has got the extra bit on the back where you can sleep...

Obviously they knew as much about lorries as they do about ballroom dancing and flower arranging, but that didn't stop them trying to justify their purchases!

James was proud of his Scania 94D. Jeremy had got hold of a massive Renault Magnum but all he could find to say about it was: "It has a flat floor and that means it's easier to fit a carpet."

As for Richard, he turned up in an ERF, which he claimed was a small, fast 'racing truck'. The others laughed!

Before the tests began, they had to go away and customise their lorries.

Richard decided to make his look more American by giving it a much longer bonnet. Unfortunately all he could find for the job was an old dog kennel!

James went for a colourful Indian look with lots of bright paint and pretty patterns, which was the exact opposite to Jeremy, who painted his whole truck in black stealth paint.

The first challenge was to see who could powerslide their truck on a skid pan. James wasn't sure: 'You can't powerslide lorries.' But as Richard pointed out, James couldn't actually powerslide *anything.*

They were given a demo by Rig Stig, another of the Stig's 'larger than life' cousins.

Look at that he's doing a **doughnut**

Gingerly, our heroes hit the skid pan. Jeremy couldn't see a thing out of his windows, which was just as well as the other two were making even more of a hash of things than he was!

Jeremy was giving it his best, but then had a nasty accident with a gear stick and had to retire hurt. In the end they all failed completely.

So James, what do you reckon... Can you **do it?**

Piece of **cake.**

Here we go, slide... **Come on**, you're a racing truck – this is what you should be **good** at!

Then his bonnet/kennel flew off.

Next they had to hitch up a trailer to their truck. Richard, who is good with farm machinery, apparently, was pretty confident.

Unfortunately, when he drove off he left the trailer behind, not once but twice, much to the others' amusement.

If a lorry driver can do **that**, why isn't he a **brain surgeon?**

With the trailers attached, thanks largely to the help of some real lorry drivers, it was off to test their driving skills on the twisty, turny Alpine handling course (the one where James Bond rolled his Aston Martin in *Casino Royale*).

I didn't **think** it would be difficult, and it's **not.**

The idea was to drive as smoothly as possible, because all three had valuable goods in their trailers. Richard had a car that wasn't fastened down, James had a giant wedding cake, while at one end of Jeremy's trailer was some straw, and at the other end an electric fire. Obviously, the **last** thing he wanted to do was catch fire...

KRUMP!

The lads were having trouble just trying to change gear.

When you **finally** reach 18th gear you get **carved up** and have to start **all over** again.

Jeremy couldn't see that well out of his stealth-black window.

Whose car?

You've **clipped** a car.

I don't know, but they **will** notice.

Eat my Magnum – **yeah!**

They finally reached the start line and in a right turn up for the books, Captain Slow was first away!

But rather than a simple race, Jezza and James set about things like a Demolition Derby, trying to bash and crash each other off the track. And they'd all forgotten about their precious cargoes.

Richard nearly turned his truck over as he careered around a sharp hairpin bend.

And then he lost his cargo, as the car crashed out of the back of his trailer while he was chugging up a hill.

Meanwhile, James had rammed Jeremy, who'd then ground to a halt half way up a hill.

James won although there wasn't a lot left of his cake.

Then Jeremy arrived – in a blaze of glory!

Moving swiftly on from what was, let's face it, an utterly useless display of lorry driving, the lads set out to see whose lorry was fastest.

Normally, HGVs are limited to just 56mph, but not for this test, which involved racing around a two-mile long bowl.

Jeremy now had what he called a 'lighter, convertible Magnum.'

You're on **fire!**

That is **actually** quite bad now.

Richard had hit 90 mph when they were suddenly told to stop. The cameraman retreated to a safe distance as tyres began to squeal.

James was a bit hard on his brakes!

SCREEEECH!

Was it really **that** frightening?

Yes.

Next was a hill start with the inevitable twist. Each truck was placed on a slope with something close to the lads' hearts placed behind them.

For Jeremy it was his drum kit. He managed to pull it off with no trouble: "The one thing a Renault Magnum can do is a hill start." Richard and James decided to wreck his drums in any case!

Then it got serious. Oliver, Richard's beloved car from the Botswana challenge, was next. But Richard couldn't go through with it and gave up.

For James, his favourite grand piano would be crushed if he got it wrong... unfortunately the legs fell off anyway as they were getting it into position! James made sure it was well and truly broken by running over it in any case.

Back in the studio, James gave the results... and for the first time in a while, Captain Slow was the winner!

You *just* **clipped it** on the way back.

It **never** moved an **inch**. You've **smashed** my drum kit!

The last challenge was a test of speed, braking and toughness, with each truck having to crash through an 'obstacle', and then stop as quickly as possible.

The person who stopped in the shortest distance would win a year's supply of pies.

With the windscreens heavily fortified, Richard went first and survived unscathed as he rammed his way through a Portakabin.

Next up was James who was faced by a mountain of 600 office water coolers.

He survived too but sailed past the mark set by Richard. And so to Jeremy in his fearsome Magnum, who had the small task of hurtling through a brick wall. The Magnum faired better than Jezza, who injured himself yet again.

What **sort** of pies?

BA-DOOM

Oh my lord!

I'm glad I'm not in **his** lorry.

Ow, this actually

AN YOU GET FOR £5000 CHALLENGE

It's **hopeless** to be honest

Hidden Gem

Here are eleven teasing questions to test the old grey matter. First solve the clues and write your answers in the grid. Next, re-arrange the letters in the shaded boxes to spell out the name of one of the show's favourites makes of car – even if it is usually a bit insane!

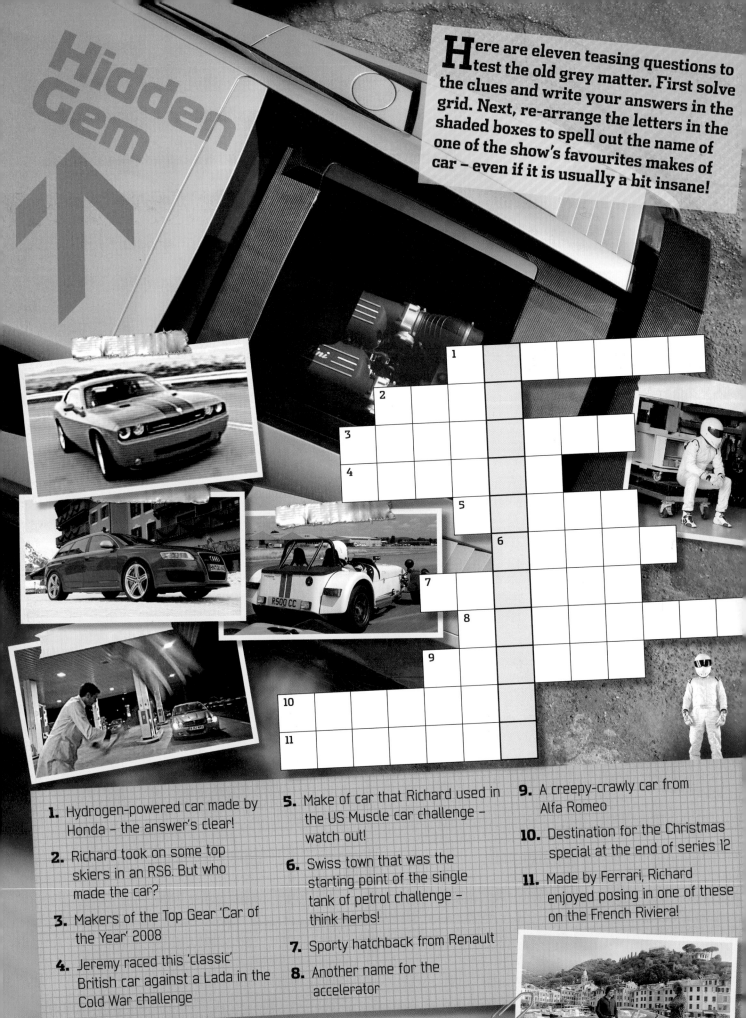

1. Hydrogen-powered car made by Honda – the answer's clear!

2. Richard took on some top skiers in an RS6. But who made the car?

3. Makers of the Top Gear 'Car of the Year' 2008

4. Jeremy raced this 'classic' British car against a Lada in the Cold War challenge

5. Make of car that Richard used in the US Muscle car challenge – watch out!

6. Swiss town that was the starting point of the single tank of petrol challenge – think herbs!

7. Sporty hatchback from Renault

8. Another name for the accelerator

9. A creepy-crawly car from Alfa Romeo

10. Destination for the Christmas special at the end of series 12

11. Made by Ferrari, Richard enjoyed posing in one of these on the French Riviera!

ROADWORKS TRUE OR FALSE?

The lads love a good moan, and what really gets their backs up are roadworks, especially ones that go on for ever yet have no one working on them!

So, with the rallying cry of 'How hard can it be?' they set about trying to speed things up. But which of these statements about the day Top Gear got its hands dirty are true?

Our resurfacing work shall last for 1000 years!

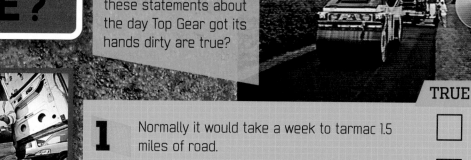

Lunch, on this job, is what you can find in the **hedge.**

If a job's worth doing, it's worth doing **quickly!**

No – **well!**

Steal their tarmac? I like your thinking!

		TRUE	FALSE
1	Normally it would take a week to tarmac 1.5 miles of road.	☐	☐
2	Jeremy and the team attempted to lay 1100 tonnes of tarmac in one day.	☐	☐
3	James calculated that in 2008 exactly 62% of the UK's road were closed at any one time because of roadworks.	☐	☐
4	Jeremy gave several motivating speeches as the lads laboured away through the night, one of which compared what they were doing to building the Great Wall of China.	☐	☐
5	Rather than take a lunch break the lads foraged for food in the hedges. Richard found and ate an old Cornish pasty that had been thrown out of a car window.	☐	☐
6	As a 'joke' Jezza threw James' mobile phone under the wheels of the steam roller.	☐	☐
7	When they arrived, Jeremy compared the pitted, bumpy road to an teenager's face.	☐	☐
8	A sticky substance called bitumen helps the tarmac stick to the road. Bitumen is made out of cheese, horse hair and boiled maggots.	☐	☐
9	A Top Gear cameraman managed to shut down the whole quarry by leaning on the Emergency Stop button.	☐	☐
10	James was sent to set up the diversion signs and got it so completely right that he was congratulated on his planning by the Minister of Transport.		☐

We're not even going to insult your intelligence by giving you a choice on this one!

FOXTAILS & MUDTRAILS

Play this board game and find out how Jeremy felt when he was chased by a load of starving hounds! Serves him right for painting his car like a fox...

The Rules

1. Throw a dice – highest roll goes first.
2. Put your coins or counters on the start, then take turns to throw a dice and move along the board.
3. When you land on a square with a fox tail, move up it. And when you get to a mud-trail – yep, you've guessed it – you have to slide down!

FINISH Phew, made it. You've out-FOXED 'em!	79	78	77
61	62	63	64
60	59	58 Come on, get out of that stream, or you're dead meat!	57
41	42	43	44
40	39	38	37 Pick up speed o open ground!
21	22 The going is very bumpy and you keep hitting your head!	23	24
20	19	18	17
START	2	3	4 Nice one, you've got a 2-minute head-start on the hounds!

Please come on! Pleeeease, I **beg** of you!

DOOFF

0-60 in 12 seconds. That's **not** fast, I admit...

75	74	I'm going to be eaten by dogs, and I'm a **pregnant** woman...	72	71 You get stuck again and phone the AA!
66	67 Time to drive with reckless speed!	73	69	70
		68		
55	54	53 DOH! You're stuck in a ditch!	52	51
46	47	48	49	50
's a stupid gate way!				**Which** wood?!?
35	34	33	32 You're lost and have to look at the map!	31
26 Confuse them by driving through some smelly flowers!	27	28	29	30
15	14 AAARGH! It's all muddy and slippery in the wood!	13	12	11
6	7 The hunt has set off and the hounds have got your scent!	8	9	10

> The acceleration is so **brutal**, I think my eyes have moved round the **side** of my head like a pigeon. **Powerrrrr!**

Pagani Zonda F Roadster

As Jeremy had hurt his neck, and Richard was busy doing adverts, James finally got to play with a supercar. The fastest, most exclusive, most powerful and most expensive roadster in the world – the Zonda F Roadster.

 Engine: 7.3 litre V12

 Power: 650bhp

 0-60mph: 3.6secs

 Max. speed: over 300kph

 TG lap time: 1min 17.8secs

Good stuff:

- Hit the carbon ceramic brakes, and it goes from 125 to a standstill in 4.4 secs. 'And my eyeballs are back in the correct position on the front of my face'
- The entire shell is naked carbon fibre, which is very strong. It's so well-engineered that it's the same weight as the Zonda with a roof

Bad stuff:

- It costs £825,000, and even if you could afford it they've sold them all
- Very, very hard to drive well unless your first name is 'The' and your surname is 'Stig'

That's as fast as I'm **ever** going to go in a car!

Bugatti Veyron

James also got to visit VW's test track and take the Bugatti Veyron up to top speed – one third the speed of sound.

 Engine: 8.0 litre W16 – think of it as two V8s side-by-side

 Power: 1001bhp

 0-60mph: 2.4secs

 Max. speed: 253.5mph. The fastest production car in the world.

 TG lap time: 1min 18.3secs – it's just too heavy to throw round this short circuit.

Good stuff:

- Four wheel drive, to get that mountain of power onto the road
- The rear wing flips up to act as an airbrake at speeds above 125mph, providing as much braking force as a normal car gets from its, er, brakes

Bad stuff:

- Weighs 2,034.8 kg – 800kg more than the Zonda
- Costs €1,100,000 – over a million pounds at current exchange rates. Even so, VW lose money on every one
- At full speed, it empties the 100-litre fuel tank in twelve minutes. And wears the tyres out in fifteen

POWER LAP TIMES

Gumpert Apollo 1.17.1

Ascari A10 1.17.3

Koenigggseggisseggnignigsegigiseggg CCX (with Top Gear spoiler) 1.17...

Pagani Zonda F Roadster 1.17.8

Bugatti Veyron 1.18.3

Pagani Zonda F 1.18.4

Maserati MC12 1.18.9

Ferrari Enzo 1.19.0

Ariel Atom 1.19.5

Lamborghini LP560 1.19.5

Ferrari 430 Scuderia 1.19.7

Nissan GTR 1.19.7

Lamborghini LP640 1.19.8

Porsche Carerra GT 1.19.8

Koenigsegg CCX 1.20.4

Ascari KZ1 1.20.7

Mercedes McLaren SLR 1.20.9

Ferrari 599GTB 1.21.2

Ford GT 1.21.9

Ferrari 360 CS 1.22.3

Porsche GT3 RS 1.22.3

Just to keep you up to date, here's the top of the Power Laps board at the end of Series 12. Who knows what could get a place here next?

It is **unbelieveably** fast.

The Atom – about a tenth the cost of an other car here!

Page 14: Beat the bunkers

Page 15: F1 Speed Merchants

1:44.6 – Nigel Mansell. 1:44.7 – Lewis Hamilton.
1:44.7 – Jenson Button. 1:46.3 – Damon Hill.
1:47.1 –Mark Webber. But none of them beat the
Stig, who got 1:44.4. Yay!

Page 18: Twelve of the best

R	E	L	M	I	A	D	M	I	N	S	A	G
O	S	T	O	R	L	A	R	T	L	E	J	T
V	M	U	G	T	O	I	T	B	E	A	M	J
R	A	I	M	D	U	M	V	R	G	S	T	A
E	S	R	O	L	L	S	R	O	Y	C	E	G
M	T	A	R	E	B	D	A	I	M	R	L	U
R	O	R	G	A	H	E	R	T	A	C	E	A
G	N	T	A	R	T	V	N	U	A	R	Y	R
A	M	I	N	I	U	I	R	T	P	O	H	V
N	A	N	U	A	R	G	E	S	L	V	T	L
T	R	O	G	U	A	R	G	A	J	E	N	R
L	T	T	A	R	H	A	M	C	T	R	Y	H
E	I	S	J	A	H	P	M	U	I	R	T	A
Y	N	A	M	O	G	R	A	N	I	T	A	M

Page 32: The Super Quiz

1: a, 2: a, 3: c, 4: b, 5: c, 6: b, 7: b, 8: b, 9: a, 10: a,
11: a, 12: a, 13: b, 14: b, 15: b.

Page 34: Modding Madness

ACROSS: 3) Tyres 6) Spoiler 8) Glass
10) Mitsubishi 11) Jeremy 12) Saw.

DOWN: 1) Studio 2) Boring 4) Suspension
5) Avantime 7) Renault 9) Chips

Page 35: Car-doku!

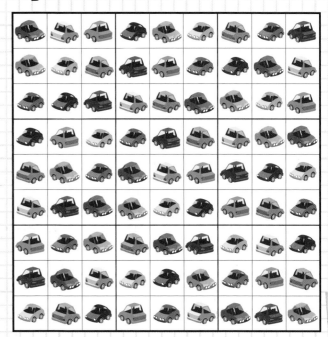

Page 54: Hidden Gem

```
        C L A R I T Y
      A U D I
    C A T E R H A M
    M A R I N A
        D O D G E
        B A S E L
      M E G A N E
        T H R O T T L E
      S P I D E R
  V I E T N A M
  D A Y T O N A
```

Answer: *Lamborghini*

Page 55: Road Repairs

1: True. 2: True. 3: False – it's bad, but not that bad!
4: True. 5: False – the Hamster's a fussy eater.
6: False – James hurled Jezza's megaphone under the
wheels, and in revenge, James' chips were crushed.
7: True – he's not known for his sensitivity. 8: False –
bitumen's made out of oil. 9: True. 10: Do me a favour!

How Many Stigs?

We counted 37. But we could be wrong...

Some say
the Stig is
rather fond of the
Nissan GTR...